THE CUSTOMER SERVICE POCKETBOOK

3rd Edition

By Sean McManus & Tony Newby

Drawings by Phil Hailstone

Published by:

Management Pocketbooks Ltd

Laurel House, Station Approach, Alresford, Hants SO24 9JH, U.K.

Tel: +44 (0)1962 735573   Fax: +44 (0)1962 733637

Email: sales@pocketbook.co.uk

Website: www.pocketbook.co.uk

Previous edition ISBN 978 1 903776 00 1

© Tony Newby (1st edition) 1991

© Sean McManus and Tony Newby 2002, 2013

This edition published 2013

ISBN 978 1 906610 55 5

E-book ISBN 978 1 908284 24 2

British Library Cataloguing-in-Publication Data – A catalogue record for this book is available from the British Library.

Design, typesetting and graphics by **efex ltd**.   Printed in U.K.

Gaers

658.812

Mauke

3005929

£8.99

CONTENTS

WHAT IS CUSTOMER SERVICE?

DEFINING CUSTOMER SERVICE

Customer service is simply another term for helping customers.

It might include:

- Helping customers to find products or services
- Advising customers on which products are most suitable for them
- Finding the answers to customer questions about your products or organisation
- Giving customers advice on how to use a product
- Helping customers to complete a purchase
- Responding to after sales queries
- Receiving and resolving complaints

WHAT IS CUSTOMER SERVICE?

PUTTING CUSTOMERS FIRST

Customer service is sometimes called customer care, because it's about looking after customers, and putting their needs first.

Good customer service is about:

- Treating customers with respect and thinking of them as people the organisation might be able to help with its products and services, rather than just 'people to be sold stuff'
- Learning what each customer needs, and helping to find products or services to satisfy those needs
- Being supportive and offering help after the sale, and not rejecting requests for help once the money is in the till
- Making customers happy with what they buy, and how they're sold it

WHAT IS CUSTOMER SERVICE?

CUSTOMER CONTACT

Customer service matters because **everybody** in **every** organisation:

- Either helps customers **directly**
- Or helps colleagues (**internal customers**) who serve the customer

This book is for people who work in:

- Businesses supplying goods or services
- Governmental and public sector organisations
- Voluntary organisations

…because they **all** have customers.

HOW IS CUSTOMER SERVICE DELIVERED?

Customer service can be delivered in lots of different ways:

- **Face to face** – when a customer visits your premises or you visit theirs
- **By telephone** – whether the customer phones you, or you phone them
- **By email** – when you enter into a one-to-one correspondence
- **By post** – increasingly rarely, but the post remains a commonly-used channel for receiving and responding to complaints, and for product delivery
- **Using social media** – such as Twitter and Facebook, to answer customer queries and offer advice

AUTOMATED CUSTOMER SERVICE

In some organisations, there might be technologies that help to automate some aspects of customer service, or that enable customers to serve themselves.

A bank, for example, might have a website that enables customers to check their balance and make payments without needing any personal assistance. A utilities company might have a website that offers answers to popular questions when a customer sends a message through it.

These tools can help to improve the customer experience, but should not be a barrier to delivering more personal service when customers need it.

Ultimately, customer service is about people (not machines) helping people.

WHICH CHANNELS DO YOU USE?

The service channel you use depends on the nature of
your business, and your customers' preferences.

A dentist, for example, might mostly use face to
face and the telephone.

A company selling office supplies to other
businesses, might use telephone and
email the most.

Often, you'll switch between channels while
serving a single customer enquiry. You might
receive a complaint in person but answer it
with a phone call when you have the facts later.
Or you might have an email correspondence that
results in you arranging to meet the customer to
teach them how to use something they've bought.

WHAT IS A CUSTOMER?

In this book, we'll use the word 'customer' to refer to anyone who might want to use your products or services, or seek help from you.

It includes:

- Individuals who have bought from you, or who are considering buying from you
- People who represent organisations that buy from you, or might do so in the future
- People who use your services, even if they don't directly pay for them, for example in the government or voluntary sectors
- Members of the public you encounter on social media, who might be interested in using your services
- Your colleagues, who are 'internal customers' and ultimately serve the external customer

You might have ten customers, or ten million, but each one is important to the future of your organisation.

WHY
CUSTOMER SERVICE MATTERS

YOUR PERSONAL NEEDS

The benefits to you personally of delivering good customer service are:

- You'll get more satisfaction, knowing that you are doing a good job, and that colleagues and customers respect you and your work
- You'll have less re-work to do if you get it right first time
  - And you will not have to answer complaints
  - So you'll waste less time 'fire-fighting' problems
  - And will have more control of your time and workload
- You'll have more opportunities for career progression too: organisations are more likely to promote people who take responsibility for delivering great service, internally or externally

ORGANISATION'S NEEDS

Businesses and non-profit organisations need:

- Sustainable competitive advantage: rival businesses might easily match your prices or products, but will find it harder to infuse the business with an outstanding customer service ethic

- A productive, stress-free work environment: great customer service means happier customers, happier team members and less conflict at work

- Cost-efficiency: satisfying customers first time means less money is wasted taking complaints and correcting mistakes. This is particularly important in public sector organisations where there is no obvious profit to track, but there can be a lot of hidden wastage

- A good reputation: this is important for attracting future customers and investors, and essential for the credibility of non-profit organisations

- Strong differentiation: good customer service frees companies from the downward spiral of competing on price because people will pay more for great service

WHY CUSTOMER SERVICE MATTERS

THE IMPORTANCE OF *HOW*

Today *how* you deliver your products and services is as important as *what* they are.

Competing goods and services don't differ greatly from each other, so customers will choose where to shop based on the service they get.

Before they consider spending any money, customers will already know whether they trust you and like you. They will have judged what you look like, what you sound like and how responsive you are. They will have seen how you treat other customers.

Often customers can only judge quality based on the service they get. How can a customer judge an accountant's competence, or a novice tell whether a computer is right for them? They all depend on customer service that inspires confidence and shows attention to their needs.

CUSTOMERS BUY EXPERIENCES

Customers buy an experience that starts when they first come into contact with you, either on your premises, on the phone or on the internet.

They might enjoy browsing your shelves or appreciate the advice of your sales team on what they might like. If they're buying a present, they'll be delighted if you offer to wrap it for them. If they buy a computer, they might value your after-sales service helping them to get it working.

Some customers will buy books online for the experience of reading reviews from other readers, and others will prefer the experience of turning the pages in a bookstore.

Everything you do for or to the customer is part of the experience they buy, and part of how you differentiate your organisation.

UNDERSTANDING CUSTOMER EXPECTATIONS

Customers have expectations that are:

- Often set by other industries, such as banks, airlines, and fast food outlets. You are competing with the most responsive organisations in every communication channel you use

- Continually evolving and growing more demanding

EXCEEDING CUSTOMER EXPECTATIONS

The aim of customer service is to make customers happy, or better still *delighted*, with the experience they have when dealing with you. To do that, you need to exceed their expectations with every contact.

If your customer service is merely *adequate*, then it is probably invisible to customers.

Only **excellent** service gets noticed!

Because expectations are always rising, your standards of customer service must be continuously improving too.

THE VALUE OF REPEAT BUSINESS

Repeat custom is the life-blood of most businesses, so every customer counts.

Even customers who make small purchases can have a large lifetime value to you. For example, a man buys some fruit on his way to work. It only costs a pound but he buys fruit every working day, making a total of £230 per year. And he buys fruit for ten years, spending £2,300 in total.

If the shopkeeper can delight him with great service, the customer will be loyal to that shop, and bring a lifetime of business. If not, that customer could be easily enticed by a competitor that makes an extra effort to keep him happy.

THE LIFETIME VALUE OF CUSTOMERS

The fruit example shows how small amounts add up, but every customer has a lifetime value. It doesn't matter whether the sale is big or small, frequent or occasional.

What might be the lifetime value of one of your customers?

Work it out like this:

- Take the average value of a sale
- Multiply it by how many times a year a customer might buy what you sell (from you, or from competitors)
- Multiply it again by how long the customer will be buying that product

If customers are that valuable, how much can the business afford to invest to win each customer? The cost of making an extra effort to help customers is always justified. If you lose a customer, you give your competitors a gift: income from that customer for life.

CREATING AMBASSADORS

If you delight customers, they will:

- Recommend you to their friends
- Write glowing reviews of your services on internet review sites
- Be loyal to you

Unprompted recommendations from satisfied customers are the most credible promotion you can have.

THE SILENT COMPLAINER

If customers are dissatisfied, they usually won't tell you.
They'll tell everybody else.

- They post negative reviews
- They tell their friends
- They add embellishments
- It turns into a real horror story – you may even attract hostile press publicity

23

THE CONNECTED CUSTOMER

People are more connected than ever before. When they share a story on a social network, it might reach 100 or 200 people who trust their judgement. If those people start to share the story, it can quickly go viral and reach thousands.

Reviews are popular online, too. They appear on sites dedicated to particular sectors (such as travel review sites), on local directory sites, and on retail sites. Customers can post a review to recommend your business or to warn others off. That means a single fleeting customer service experience can have a lasting impact on your business.

Customers increasingly consult reviews from other customers before buying, and search engines can dredge up a review years after it was written.

WHY CUSTOMER SERVICE MATTERS

CASE STUDY

Canadian musician Dave Carroll found his guitar was damaged when he flew with United Airlines, and other passengers on his flight said they saw baggage handlers throwing guitars.

He tried to get compensation from the airline for nine months without success ...

CASE STUDY

... So he wrote and recorded a country song called 'United Breaks Guitars', which complains about the indifferent customer service he received. He posted a video for the song on YouTube, and within a day, it was watched 150,000 times. To date, it's been played over 13 million times.

For United Airlines, one customer complaint became a public relations disaster.

The company then contacted the customer to resolve his complaint and asked for permission to use the video in training, so it could work on changing its culture.

DELIVERING
GREAT CUSTOMER SERVICE

DELIVERING GREAT CUSTOMER SERVICE

WHAT YOU NEED

To deliver good customer service, you will need:

- Good quality products and services
- Consistent and accurate information on products, orders, customers, and the organisation. You can't know or remember everything, but you should be able to find it out
- A good understanding of the products or services you supply and the needs of external customers, so you can match them up
- A thorough knowledge of the systems, procedures and teams in your organisation
- Reliable systems and suppliers

DELIVERING GREAT CUSTOMER SERVICE

PERSONAL QUALITIES REQUIRED

To deliver good customer service, you will also need these personal qualities:

- A positive attitude, with dedication to getting it right first time, and a commitment to helping colleagues
- Attention to detail
- A willingness to take responsibility
- The confidence to stay calm under pressure
- Excellent communication skills

DELIVERING GREAT CUSTOMER SERVICE

QUALITY

Good customer service is about:

- The quality of what you deliver; and
- The quality of how you deliver it

Quality isn't an abstract notion of how good something is. It's about how appropriate something is for your customers' needs, and how well it meets their expectations.

A carrier bag and a rucksack can both be high-quality bags, because they satisfy different needs.

Quality is about making sure you're delivering the right things to the right people at the right time.

DELIVERING GREAT CUSTOMER SERVICE

A POSITIVE ATTITUDE

To deliver good customer service, you need to have a 'can do' attitude, and be willing to help customers and colleagues.

It's challenging at times, but every query or complaint is an opportunity to delight a customer, and create a company ambassador.

DELIVERING GREAT CUSTOMER SERVICE

ATTENTION TO DETAIL

Good customer service is the product of close attention to important small details.

For example:

- A shop assistant who remembers a customer's favourite magazine and tells her when a new issue comes out
- An unprompted phone call to check that the customer is happy
- A restaurant where the waiters can advise customers who have an allergy to certain ingredients

Conversely, bad customer service often results from poor attention to names, numbers, dates, orders and other details.

Most of the improvements needed to achieve excellent customer service require very small changes in the way we work day-to-day.

DELIVERING GREAT CUSTOMER SERVICE

TAKING RESPONSIBILITY

When customers turn to you for help, they want to know that you will take responsibility for getting them what they need.

Sometimes you might be let down by tools or suppliers, but it's still **your** responsibility to satisfy your customers, and find a solution.

You might deliver service across multiple channels, and customers expect to be able to switch between them at will. They want to pop into a shop as they're passing, send a message through your social media page, or pick up the phone. Their choice of channel might not be ideal for the organisation, but whoever receives the enquiry is responsible for getting it to someone who can help.

Customers want to work with a single, harmonious company. If you can't help them, you are responsible for finding the people who can.

DELIVERING GREAT CUSTOMER SERVICE

INSPIRING CONFIDENCE

Give customers confidence that you are taking responsibility:

- Be prepared to apologise on behalf of the company if mistakes have been made

- Introduce yourself by name on the phone, or wear a name badge so customers know you're accountable

- Help customers to navigate your organisation. Introduce them to the right person to help, or show them to the shelves where the products they need are kept

- Offer to follow up personally. Give your name and number. Customers want consistency in their dealings with the company, and prefer not to explain their situation again to someone new

- Tell customers what you're doing. Give them confidence that any delays they suffer are because you're trying to help them

HOW TO DELIGHT CUSTOMERS

It's easy to think of ways to delight customers, but the important thing is that your surprises meet their needs. For example:

- If a customer buys an expensive and cumbersome table, will they be more impressed if they're given a 5% discount or if the sales team spends half an hour helping them to get it into their car? The cost to the company might be the same, but the impact on the customer will be very different

- If a shop doesn't stock something the customer needs, it can still leave an impression of good service. Imagine how pleased customers would feel if the shop recommended another company to help them. The shop has helped create a future buyer by offering great service to a browser. Remember, the shop couldn't have made the sale and the customer had to go to a competitor anyway

How can you delight your customers?

GREAT CUSTOMER SERVICE

There are examples of great customer service all around us, which can inspire us. Here are some I've spotted:

- At John Lewis, they have a central service desk where an assistant takes your name and query, and then finds a sales assistant who can help you. You don't have to try to find free staff on the shop floor, and the team takes responsibility for finding someone with expertise in the products you're looking at

- Air Asia keeps racks of umbrellas that passengers can use to shelter from the rain as they walk across the tarmac, from the airport to the plane. A small touch like this can result in a much more comfortable flight, and make customers feel more appreciated

- My mobile phone company noticed when I tried to call a couple of times and couldn't get through, and it automatically texted me an apology and a £5 credit on my bill

(36) What examples of great customer service have you come across?

REFLECTING ON CUSTOMER SERVICE

Think of one occasion in the last six months when you have received excellent customer service and one occasion when the service was terrible.

For each example, ask yourself:

- How do you think you were regarded by the person serving you?
- How did you feel about the service you received?
- What were your expectations, and how well did the service meet them?
- What was the best or worst thing about the service you received?
- How likely are you to use that organisation again?
- What would you say to friends about that organisation?

REFLECTING ON CUSTOMER SERVICE

Think about all your experiences as a customer:

- How do you want organisations to make you feel when you're dealing with them?
- What do you find annoying or irritating in customer service you've received?
- What makes you happy in customer service you've received?

How can you use your personal experiences of customer service to better understand what your own customers want, and how your organisation can keep its customers happy?

EFFECTIVE CUSTOMER COMMUNICATIONS

WHY COMMUNICATION MATTERS

Customer service always involves communicating with customers or colleagues, so good communication skills are vital if you are to deliver great service.

Communication skills include:

- Listening to customers and colleagues, so you can find out what they need from you and how you can help
- Talking to customers, so you can give them information they need, explain how you're helping them, or reassure them if they've had a bad experience
- Writing to customers, in response to emails, letters or social media messages you have received

EFFECTIVE CUSTOMER COMMUNICATIONS

DEVELOPING LISTENING SKILLS

1. THE 80:20 RATIO

Effective listening means not talking.

- They talk, you listen – the ratio should be 80:20 or even 90:10
- You don't interrupt (unless they are way off the subject, or you can't understand what they are saying)
- You pay attention to what they are saying, rather than pretending to listen while you plan what you'll say next
- You make written notes of key points

EFFECTIVE CUSTOMER COMMUNICATIONS

DEVELOPING LISTENING SKILLS

2. CHECKING UNDERSTANDING

Check that you have understood what has been said.

- Ask questions to clarify anything you are unsure about
- From time to time give a reflective summary, which briefly paraphrases what the other person has been saying
- Don't *tune out* the things that you might be less pleased to hear

EFFECTIVE CUSTOMER COMMUNICATIONS

DEVELOPING LISTENING SKILLS

3. DEMONSTRATING LISTENING

Demonstrate that you are listening.

- **Eye contact** – maintain frequent contact, without giving the impression of a fixed stare
- **Body language** – be comfortable, not stiff; open rather than with defensively-crossed arms; lean slightly towards the person, without threatening their sense of personal space
- **Interested tone of voice** – whatever the words you use, if you don't mean what you say, your tone will give away your insincerity

If you are genuinely interested in helping customers, the body language will flow naturally.

DEVELOPING LISTENING SKILLS

4. BUILDING RELATIONSHIPS

Build the relationship with the other person.

- Give them space to let off steam if they need to, before you move into a problem-solving mode

- Show that you can see things from their point of view

- Focus on positive action for the future, rather than raking over history

- Include them as contributors to your planned actions – 'We can sort this out together…'

EFFECTIVE CUSTOMER COMMUNICATIONS

DEVELOPING LISTENING SKILLS

5. DIAGNOSTIC LISTENING

Treat listening as a diagnostic process.

- Where errors have occurred, resist the urge to argue, to defend or to excuse
- Admit mistakes and apologise sincerely, even if you personally had nothing to do with causing the problem – as far as a customer is concerned, you represent everybody in the organisation
- Even if the request or the problem sounds familiar, don't jump to conclusions before you have gathered all the facts
- Work out what the customer would ideally like you to do for them
- Look for solutions, not obstacles
- Share what you learn with others in your organisation, so it can more closely meet customers' needs in the future

EFFECTIVE CUSTOMER COMMUNICATIONS

TALKING POINTS

When you need to speak to customers, use these tips:

- **Smile!** – when you speak with a smile, it can even be heard over the phone
- **How can I help you?** – bring customers promptly to the point by asking them how you can help
- **Listen** – remember to actively listen to what customers say
- **Speak clearly and don't speak too quickly** – remember the goal is to make sure the customer understands what you're saying. If the customer is annoyed it can be particularly difficult to remain clear and calm, but it's essential
- **Use a clear phone line** – if you have a poor mobile connection, find an alternative or offer to call back later. To deliver good service, you need to be heard, and need confidence you have understood the customer and have been understood yourself

EFFECTIVE CUSTOMER COMMUNICATIONS

GETTING YOUR POINT ACROSS

No matter which channel you are using to communicate with a customer or colleague, to make sure your message is understood, your communication should be:

- **Friendly** – smile and start with a friendly greeting. In business to business trade, it's increasingly common to use first names when dealing with people

- **Attentive** – when you're listening to a customer or talking to them, focus your complete attention on them. If you're distracted, try to eliminate the distraction, by taking the phone somewhere quieter, for example

- **Convenient** – before starting a lengthy conversation, check whether the other person has time for it, or ask to schedule time. Don't let the communication suffer because one person needs to hurry it

- **Respectful** – communications are increasingly informal, but you should remain polite and respectful of the customer

- **Tailored** – personalise your message to the customer's requirements and knowledge level (don't bamboozle them with jargon, or tell them things they already know)

EFFECTIVE CUSTOMER COMMUNICATIONS

GETTING YOUR POINT ACROSS
THE ELEMENTS OF COMMUNICATION

There are four main elements to communication:

- **Purpose** – what you are aiming to achieve by communicating
- **Content** – what the substance of your message consists of
- **Presentation** – the way in which you present your message
- **Style** – the manner in which you express yourself

To get your message across, you need to make sure
you're using the right content, presentation and
style for your purpose.

EFFECTIVE CUSTOMER COMMUNICATIONS

GETTING YOUR POINT ACROSS
PURPOSE

We communicate with other people in order to:

- Give them information they need
- Ask them for information we need
- Make recommendations or suggestions (to persuade)
- Request action by the other person

Sometimes, only one of these purposes applies, at other times a single written message or conversation might cover several purposes.

When you reflect on your purpose in making the communication, you can begin to think about the best way to express what you want (through the channel you use, the tone you adopt, your choice of words, and so on).

GETTING YOUR POINT ACROSS
CONTENT

Communication skills are largely about how you interact with people, but it's important to have the right message too.

That means being:

- **Honest** – customers will know if you're trying to fob them off, and will have more respect for you and the organisation if you can admit weaknesses and work with them to resolve any problems

- **Accurate** – it's important that the information you share is right, so that any decisions you or the customer make are based on reality. Customers would usually prefer that you double check something if you're not certain

- **Timely** – the right information at the wrong time is useless. Understanding when customers need something is as important as knowing what they need. They might have a deadline, such as a birthday when present buying. Being timely often means being proactive, by phoning a customer when a new delivery arrives, for example

- **Consistent** – conflicting information causes enormous frustration

EFFECTIVE CUSTOMER COMMUNICATIONS

GETTING YOUR POINT ACROSS

CONTENT

- **Concise** – decide what is essential and what is irrelevant – and leave out the inessentials! Get to the point quickly, too

- **Complete** – don't be brief at the expense of the customer's understanding. If something needs explaining, do so fully. When responding to customers, make sure you've answered all their questions and addressed all their concerns

- **Focused** – the most powerful communications are those that cover a single subject. If you do have to address a few points in a written message, give each its own paragraph to make sure it stands out. Avoid writing emails and letters that ramble on and on – readers often forget one of the points in them. Swamping customers and colleagues with separate emails or letters for each query can be annoying, though, so if there are lots of different issues to resolve, consider arranging a phone call or meeting instead

- **Clear** – customers should fully understand what action you've taken, and what action you would like them to take

EFFECTIVE CUSTOMER COMMUNICATIONS

GETTING YOUR POINT ACROSS
CONTENT: STRUCTURING MESSAGES

If you're sending a written message to someone, here is a structure you can adapt for your message:

- **Greeting** (formal or informal, as appropriate) – 'Dear Mr Jones' or 'Dear George'
- **Summary** (explain why you're writing) – 'I've just received your order, and I have a few questions before I can process it.'
- **Information** (share any information you need to communicate) – 'I'm pleased to tell you that we've expanded our team, so we can bring your delivery date forward.'
- **Tell customer what you'd like them to do** – 'Please could you reply to let me know your availability for delivery in October, and your colour preference, which was missing from the order form.'
- **Offer further help** – 'Please feel free to contact me if I can clarify anything or you would like more information on your order.'
- **Sign off with thanks** – 'Thank you for your help.'
- **End with your name** (be accountable) – 'Best regards, [your name].'

EFFECTIVE CUSTOMER COMMUNICATIONS

GETTING YOUR POINT ACROSS
CONTENT: STRUCTURING REPLIES

If you're responding to a letter or an email, here's a structure you can adapt for your reply, with some example text:

- **Greeting** (formal or informal, as appropriate) – 'Dear Mrs Jones' or 'Dear Sue'
- **Thank you** – 'Thank you for bringing this to my attention.'
- **Apologise** (if necessary) – 'I'm sorry to hear about the difficulties you've been having with…'
- **Or express delight** – 'I'm delighted to hear about your experience with…'
- **Show understanding of the issue** – '… the range offered by our Christmas toy collection.'
- **Explain what happened** (if necessary) – 'Unfortunately, on this occasion, we were let down by a supplier.'

EFFECTIVE CUSTOMER COMMUNICATIONS

GETTING YOUR POINT ACROSS
CONTENT: STRUCTURING REPLIES

- **Detail the action you will take** – 'Following your feedback, we have changed supplier to avoid this problem recurring, and have retrained our staff so they can better monitor stock levels in the future.' or 'I've shared this with our customer service team, as an example of the great service we should always aspire to deliver.'

- **Tell customer what you'd like them to do** – 'If you could email me your address, please, I will arrange for a replacement for you.'

- **Offer further help** – 'Please feel free to contact me if I can offer any help in the future.'

- **Sign off with thanks** – 'Thank you for your understanding.' or 'Thank you again for sharing your experience with us.'

- **End with your name** (be accountable) – 'Best regards, [your name].'

EFFECTIVE CUSTOMER COMMUNICATIONS

GETTING YOUR POINT ACROSS

PRESENTATION

Good presentation will enhance your content by making it easy for readers to navigate and understand. Here are some tips:

- Give emails a clear descriptive subject line, and letters a short title underneath the greeting, for example – 'Revised Christmas delivery dates'

- Use a new paragraph for each idea. Paragraphs can have several sentences, all related to the same idea

- If you need to send a longer letter, use subheadings where appropriate to group related paragraphs and make it easy for readers to skim-read the main ideas and quickly get an overview of the document. Consider, though, whether you should be meeting instead of writing if the document is this complex

- Be consistent in your presentation. Too many text styles and colours make your work look clumsy and chaotic

- Check any spelling that you are unsure about. Don't depend on automatic spellcheckers to get it right. Good spelling shows care and professionalism

- If you have website links in your message, check they work

GETTING YOUR POINT ACROSS

STYLE

Your writing style should be clear and easy to understand.

- Use short sentences and plain English rather than a 'flowery' or 'literary' style

- Do not use technical jargon and in-house abbreviations that the reader is unlikely to understand; if a word has to be used that might not be understood, give a short explanation of the word the first time you use it

- Be consistent: Wherever you have a choice (such as with how dates are written or with optional spellings), use one style all the time

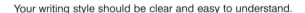

- Avoid ambiguity by using correct grammar, but don't be a slave to obsolete rules that make your writing look old-fashioned

- Choose your words precisely. Remember that tone is hard to judge in emails and social media messages, so don't over-react to incoming messages and make sure your outgoing messages are not open to misinterpretation

EFFECTIVE CUSTOMER COMMUNICATIONS

USING SOCIAL MEDIA

Social media is an important channel for communicating with customers today, and has some unique challenges.

Remember these additional points when using social media:

- **It's public** – both your messages and your customers' are shared in public where anyone can read them and share them. Keep your communications calm and clear, so there are no misunderstandings
- **Don't get defensive** – it doesn't reflect well on the organisation if you belittle or deny the customer's allegations. Accept that the customer's point of view is valid and is a fair reflection of their experience and feelings
- **Correct mistakes** – if somebody shares inaccurate information about your organisation or services, it's okay to correct or clarify that

EFFECTIVE CUSTOMER COMMUNICATIONS

USING SOCIAL MEDIA

- **Demonstrate service** – if possible, publicly share how you are resolving any complaints

- **Take it private** – if there is a serious problem, you can acknowledge that you are helping the customer in the public forum and then communicate with them privately to resolve the issue. Social networks typically have a way to message people privately, or you could use email

- **Be formal** – you might not have room to be verbose, but don't use text speak, smileys or other informal abbreviations. They can be confusing and can seem excessively relaxed and disrespectful, especially when responding to complaints. Use proper English, and send a couple of separate messages if necessary

EFFECTIVE CUSTOMER COMMUNICATIONS

USING SOCIAL MEDIA

- **Help others too** – other people will have similar issues, and might come across the social media discussion many months later. Post helpful web links or provide your customer service contact details for anyone else who has a similar issue

- **Acknowledge** – even if no response is required (such as when customers praise your service), acknowledge every message, and share important lessons with your colleagues. Remember, your competitors and customers can see this information too

EFFECTIVE CUSTOMER COMMUNICATIONS

USING EMAIL

Email is often the most convenient channel for you and the customer. Use these tips to make it work well for you:

- Think before you hit send! Email has speeded up written communication, but sometimes it's better to take time to formulate a more careful response

- Cool off before responding to email that makes you angry. Misunderstandings can arise because email has no indication of mood. Clarify what the sender intended before you reply

- Respond to customer emails promptly. If there will be a significant delay, send an email to reassure customers that you will respond

- If you have to forward an email to someone else to respond to, tell the originator what you're doing, perhaps by copying them on the forwarded message

- Don't write anything in an email that you wouldn't want to see in the papers! Emails are easily forwarded and shared

EFFECTIVE CUSTOMER COMMUNICATIONS

AVOIDING TECHNOLOGY FRUSTRATIONS

Technology can help to deliver great customer service, but you should take care that it doesn't become a source of customer dissatisfaction.

Customers will get frustrated if:

- They can't reply to your messages
- They can't navigate your call management system, get disconnected after working through the menus because nobody is available, or can't find a real person to speak to
- Complaints are registered in the database, but are never followed up
- Information you hold about customers is sold to other companies, or made available for junk-mailing them. As technology makes it easier to aggregate data on people, everyone is becoming more concerned about privacy

EFFECTIVE CUSTOMER COMMUNICATIONS

AVOIDING TECHNOLOGY FRUSTRATIONS

Customers will get frustrated if:

- They receive unhelpful standard messages, which obviously haven't been written for them or especially well selected for them

- Technology is used as an excuse for not offering service.
  Don't say 'the computer won't let me do that', and make sure you know the back-up plan so the business can still function if the technology fails

Computer says no!

EFFECTIVE CUSTOMER COMMUNICATIONS

MANAGING EXPECTATIONS

You can improve customer satisfaction by managing expectations around service delivery. First, make sure you understand what the customer's needs are, especially with regard to quality, price and timescales. Then communicate clearly, so they understand what you offer, and don't suffer disappointment later.

- Be open about the quality, size and other aspects of products or services you sell
- Tell customers honestly how long an order will take; notify them if there's a delay
- Use automatic responders to reassure a customer that an email has arrived and tell them when to expect a reply
- Use a phone system that tells holding customers how many people are ahead of them in the queue
- Disclose all fees and charges up-front. Customers are increasingly intolerant of booking fees, postage fees, credit card fees, check-in fees and other add-ons that artificially inflate the price

If you make reasonable promises, and keep them, customers need never be disappointed.

MAKING SERVICE VISIBLE

For customers, the organisation is like a black box. From the outside, they can't see your customer service processes, and it's hard to tell the difference between something you can't see and something that isn't there.

If you don't keep customers informed about what you're doing, they will believe they have been ignored.

Ideally, your organisation's processes should build in notifications that keep customers informed. An email could be sent when an order is shipped, for example, or a phone call placed to arrange delivery when a product reaches the warehouse.

If you're working outside of a formal process, make sure you communicate regularly to tell customers what you're doing, how their query is progressing, and what the next steps are. Even if you don't have good news yet, customers will be reassured to hear you've been working on their case and are still doing so.

EFFECTIVE CUSTOMER COMMUNICATIONS

WHICH CHANNEL?

Often, you can choose to deliver service face to face, by phone, by email, by post, or on social media.

The best channel to use is usually:
- The most convenient for the customer, if you're initiating contact. Ask each customer how they prefer to be contacted, and use their preference
- The channel the customer used to contact you. Reply to a letter with a letter, an email with an email, and a phone message with a phone call

Don't get locked into using one communication channel if it is no longer the best way to deal with a particular enquiry, though:
- If you need to discuss a lengthy report, email might be best so that you can insert comments in the report
- If you need to discuss something which customers feel strongly about, it's better to arrange to meet them or to speak to them

You can only change the channel with the customer's consent, so ask if they mind, and explain how you can serve them better using a different channel.

CHOOSING CHANNELS

When exercising a choice of channel, it's important to know their strengths and weaknesses.

Channel	Strengths	Weaknesses
Face to face	• Builds the most rapport • Easy to ask questions • Immediate feedback from the customer • Usually takes place at planned times or during business hours	• Usually requires travel (from you or the customer) • Can be stressful when handling complaints • Usually takes more of your time
Phone	• Using mobile phones, enables highly personalised service to be delivered from anywhere to anywhere • Can build good rapport • Easy to ask questions and get feedback	• Customers expect people to be always available on the other end of the phone • Can result in telephone tag, where people leave messages and keep missing each other • Customers dislike phone queues and menus

EFFECTIVE CUSTOMER COMMUNICATIONS

CHOOSING CHANNELS

Channel	Strengths	Weaknesses
Email	• Immediate delivery • Good for complex messages • Good for information that requires no response (such as shipping notifications) • Recipients can read and respond to messages when it is convenient for them	• Difficult to judge the tone of the message • Customers can overlook emails, or they might be blocked by spam filters

CHOOSING CHANNELS

Channel	Strengths	Weaknesses
Post	• Shows greater care • Works for customers without email	• Slow to create and deliver • Relatively expensive
Social media	• Opportunity to demonstrate great service in public • Often convenient for customers	• Complaints are seen in public

Turning complaints into opportunities

TURNING COMPLAINTS INTO OPPORTUNITIES

HEAD IN THE SAND

Some companies believe that if they make it hard to complain, customers will give up trying. They're burying their head in the sand, believing that if they can't see trouble, trouble can't find them.

You can gain a brief escape from complaints if your switchboard is continually jammed, or the *right* person is always unavailable. But sooner or later the customer will win – perhaps in dramatic form, when you find yourself profiled on TV or the company chairman is asked embarrassing questions at the AGM or (for public sector organisations) when someone writes to their MP.

What is more, the harder you make it for the complaint to get through, the more steamed up and the less inclined to compromise the customer will be when they do find you.

Customers who can't complain to you to get their problems fixed will go on to tell everyone else how bad you are instead.

TURNING COMPLAINTS INTO OPPORTUNITIES

BENEFITS OF COMPLAINTS

Complaints are an opportunity to delight a customer and correct problems that might be causing *silent complainers* and bad reviews online.

Make it easy for customers to complain and you'll be able to correct problems before you develop a reputation for bad service.

Ideally, the same complaint should only occur once because once it has arisen its cause is eliminated by:

- Improving procedures
- Eliminating product and service defects
- Improving customer service behaviour
- Setting higher performance standards
- Focusing the organisation more on customers' needs

ENCOURAGING FEEDBACK

Encourage customers to approach you with feedback and complaints, for example, by:

- Handing out postage-paid feedback forms
- Setting up a toll-free phone line
- Being visible and active on social media channels
- Advertising an email address for customer service queries
- Following up with customers after service delivery to check they are happy

If you can discover that a customer is unhappy, you have a chance to help them and make them happy, before they can damage your reputation.

CUSTOMER NEEDS

When customers have their complaints resolved satisfactorily, they tend to become stronger long-term customers than people who have not had cause to complain. The reason is simple: they are won over by the care and attention given to their complaint. Often organisations have their first chance to show a customer their exceptional care when they handle a complaint, and customers are impressed at how this contrasts with the indifference and hostility they find at other companies.

Most customers who have a complaint about something your organisation has done, or failed to do, simply want the matter put right.

In the case of a purchase that has in some way gone wrong, they also want the reassurance that they did not make a bad decision in the first place.

Most customers only become irritated, angry or even abusive when their initial attempts to get the matter put right have led them nowhere.

REMOVING COMMON CAUSES OF COMPLAINTS

Here are some common sources of complaint. Do they arise in your organisation? What can the organisation as a whole, and you personally, do to prevent them cropping up again?

- **Products or services that do not live up to the purchaser's expectations**
  Sometimes this is because customers have been sold the wrong thing, and sometimes it is because marketing materials inflate the customer's expectations in a way that the product can't support

- **Inflexibility**
  Especially regarding when and how services are delivered to the customer. Do you require customers to take a day's holiday so you can deliver to them? Can you rush through a short-notice delivery for your best customer once in a while?

- **Mistakes**
  Mistakes will always happen, but some organisations don't plan enough time to do things correctly, so they often go wrong

REMOVING COMMON CAUSES OF COMPLAINTS

- **Poor external communications**
  Can customers easily reach someone who can help them?

- **Poor internal communications**
  Communication breakdowns within the company create the impression that nobody knows what they are doing, nobody is responsible for anything, and nobody cares

- **Delays**
  Meet the deadlines you promise customers for delivering goods or responding to enquiries

TURNING COMPLAINTS INTO OPPORTUNITIES

HANDLING COMPLAINTS

- Always respond promptly and helpfully
- Identify yourself and take responsibility for solving the customer's problem. Anyone in the organisation could receive a complaint, through any communications channel. If you can't help someone directly, take responsibility for helping them find the right person in the organisation and for making sure that person responds. Never use the blocking excuse that 'It's not my job/my department'. Customer service is everyone's department
- Ask for the facts and check that you've heard them accurately
- Find out how customers would like their complaint resolved. Some might want a refund or replacement, while others might just want to register their concern

HANDLING COMPLAINTS

- Admit mistakes and apologise for them; resist the urge to blame other departments or the computer or *company policy*. Let the customer go on believing that they are dealing with one, unified organisation and not a medieval battleground of warring fiefdoms!

- Only make promises you are confident the organisation can deliver on. Your personal reputation is at stake, as well as the organisation's

- Reassure the customer about the qualities of the product or service your organisation provides once the problem has been sorted out. This is made much easier and more credible by the excellent manner in which you have just dealt with the complaint

- Share what you learn with your colleagues about how to improve the service you offer

HANDLING COMPLAINTS

DON'T

- **Don't** get defensive or argue about complaints. Agree that the problem exists and put yourself on their side: 'Let's see what we can do to sort this out'. Politely obtain the customer's name and use it

- **Don't** make the customer repeat their complaint. If you have to transfer their complaint to someone else, either in person or on the phone, show the customer you've been listening by summarising the problem for your colleague

- **Don't** leave customers waiting in the office or holding on the phone too long. Tell them what you are doing, and get someone to call them back if nobody can help now

- **Don't** tell them what you *can't* do for them. Emphasise what you *can* do

- **Don't** let reasonable complaints escalate into life-and-death dramas

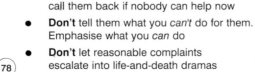

ANGRY CUSTOMERS

Customers depend on your business to deliver products or services they need and sometimes they will get angry if mistakes occur. They might feel they have wasted their time or money, or might have missed an important deadline because of your product or service failure. They might experience frustration reporting the complaint to you if they're left waiting for a response for a long time, or they're passed around the organisation endlessly.

You need to address two different problems:

- What went wrong
- How the customer feels about what went wrong

You'll need to show the customer that you are listening and sympathetic to how they feel before you can address what went wrong.

HOW TO DEFUSE CUSTOMERS

- Try to keep a calm tone of voice

- Give the customer space to let off steam before you try to steer them towards a discussion of the facts – they're probably more anxious about the situation than you are. They might have had previous enquiries mishandled

- Don't take it personally; usually it's the company that they are angry with – and as far as the customer is concerned, you are the company. They don't know you as the nice person your family and friends are familiar with

- If the customer is abusive and you can't steer the conversation onto how you can solve the problem, consider seeking help from a senior colleague

- If the customer won't calm down and they've caught you unprepared, agree to look into the problem and tell them when you'll call or email them. The customer will have time to cool down, and you will have time to formulate a response

- Suggest they contact an area manager or head office if you can't help them any further. Demonstrate confidence by giving them the contact details they need. Don't let it seem as if you are just getting rid of them

IS THE CUSTOMER ALWAYS RIGHT?

It's an old saying in customer service circles that the customer is always right, but is it really true?

- Frustrated customers might embellish their stories about bad service. Ask for specific details when they make a claim about bad service, so you can clarify what's really gone wrong

- Is it right that customers can become abusive and the company's representatives must listen to it? Staff need to know they have the management's full backing in being assertive when handling abusive complaints, and are at liberty to ask the customers to leave if they can't be calmed down

- Some customers are so angry that nothing you can do will satisfy them. Companies must be prepared to lose these customers. If a customer can't be helped by your business, both the customer and your business are better off if they take their custom elsewhere

TURNING COMPLAINTS INTO OPPORTUNITIES

STRESS

An uncomfortable side effect of dealing with angry customers is that their anger often creates stress for the person on the receiving end. Persistent stress can harm your health so it is well worth learning how to manage any stress you experience. It will help you to stay confident and to deal more effectively with the situation – and it will leave you feeling better afterwards.

To alleviate stress:

- Talk through the complaint with a colleague or friend
- After handling a difficult customer, take a moment or two to unwind; don't rush straight into the next customer
- Look after your health, with sensible exercise and eating habits
- Learn breathing exercises that will calm your stress levels

EMPOWERING GREAT CUSTOMER SERVICE

EVERYONE PLAYS A ROLE

You can empower the organisation to deliver great customer service:

- Team members throughout the company are linked in a chain that ultimately serves the customer

- Team members at all levels have information that will help colleagues perform their jobs or satisfy customers better

- By delivering great service you set a good example for other team members

- A good customer service reputation is the result of lots of small improvements in how everyone does their job and not one sudden transformation

EMPOWERING GREAT CUSTOMER SERVICE

LEADING GREAT SERVICE

Team managers should:

- Communicate clearly the organisation's and the team's strategy and priorities
- Empower team members to be flexible in helping customers, such as by offering discounts to compensate for mistakes or by agreeing unusually quick (but realistic) turnarounds for important customers on a deadline
- Ensure the lessons from customer complaints are communicated throughout the team so that products, processes and customer service can be improved
- Recognise and reward great customer service within the team
- Offer feedback and training when customer service levels fall short
- Ensure that company policies, processes and technologies don't sabotage the team's efforts to be responsive to customers

INTERNAL CUSTOMERS

Whether or not you deal with the organisation's external customers, your colleagues are your internal customers. They depend on your responsiveness and quality to deliver great service to their colleagues or the external customer.

It's helpful to think of your customer service network as consisting of a series of inputs and outputs, with yourself at the centre. Various things get passed to you (such as information, work tasks and queries) and you in turn pass your work or communications to others in the chain, or straight to the external customer.

Take a moment to think about who is in your internal customer network, and what it is that gets passed along the service chain.

- Who passes work, queries or information to you?
- Who do you pass work, queries or information to?
- What happens if there's a delay in your inputs, or if you are late passing things on to others?
- What is the ultimate impact on the external customer?

WHEN THE CHAIN WEAKENS

The internal customer chain works when everyone pulls in the same direction and there are no weak links. But it's bad news when 'us and them' barriers start to develop, such as:

- Between the sections in a process chain (where different people handle different stages of a document, for instance)
- Between head office and branches
- Between sales and marketing
- Between marketing and manufacturing

IDENTIFYING NIGGLES

Think about any times when colleagues have failed to give you the kind of service that you should get as their internal customer – incidents that have made it harder for you to do your job properly.

- It may be things you would prefer them not to do
- It may be things they don't do, but you wish they would
- It may be things that you would like them to do differently

EMPOWERING GREAT CUSTOMER SERVICE

IDENTIFYING NIGGLES

Ask yourself:

- Do the problems come from a difference of opinion over the right way to do things?
- Are the problems being magnified because you don't know the individuals you are dealing with, so you tend to assume the worst of them?
- Are there misunderstandings because you don't really know what other departments do (or are allowed to do)?
- Which items on your lists can (at least in theory) be improved?
- What would be the benefits to the organisation and yourself if these improvements were made?
- What would it take to achieve each of those improvements?

STRENGTHENING THE CHAIN

Now you've thought about the weak areas, let's think about how the chain can be strengthened. First, think about how you can improve your outputs. Close attention to small details adds up to a high quality of service. For instance:

- Responding to people without being chased by them (as easy as putting a date in your diary and placing a phone call; takes maybe five minutes)
- Keeping colleagues informed about what's happening on a project (could this really be as simple as copying them on an email and yet be so effective?)
- Arriving on time for meetings (so that other people don't waste their time waiting for you)

Think about the improvements you could ask your internal customers to give you in their service too. Point out how the organisation benefits and how getting it right first time means they have less work to do in the long run, not more! Sometimes there are good reasons why work can't be delivered to your ideal specification, but talking to your colleagues to find out why will at least stop you blaming them for inefficiency and improve your working relationship.

EMPOWERING GREAT CUSTOMER SERVICE

PASSING ON WORK

This has probably already surfaced as a source of problems in your internal network. Even if it hasn't, it is such a central element of the internal customer chain that it is worth listing some guidelines for giving (and receiving) a five-star service when you pass work on to your colleagues.

You can offer better service by:

- Negotiating deadlines and the handover of work, and not just *dumping it on someone's desk*

- Delegating full responsibility for solving a problem so that your colleague can decide the best way to handle it. Don't just dictate a series of tasks you've identified as the solution

- Being prompt in forwarding the work so that your colleague has as much time as possible to process it

- Indicating clearly and truthfully how urgent or important the work is so that your colleague can prioritise their workload

PASSING ON WORK

You can offer better service by:

- Making sure all the necessary information is sent and can be easily understood, so that people don't have to keep coming back to you for clarification, and customers don't have to repeatedly explain what they've already told you

- Making sure everything is correct before you send it on. If you inherit errors from someone else, make sure they're fixed before the work goes further

- Making sure work is sent to someone who can help, so it isn't delayed while it is repeatedly forwarded around the company (this happens especially with email enquiries)

- Making realistic promises to others about response times, so that the recipient of the work isn't put under unreasonable pressure

- Offering to help with any further information or clarification your colleague needs

MEASURING
CUSTOMER SERVICE

MEASURING CUSTOMER SERVICE

SETTING STANDARDS

Standards offer a yardstick by which the quality of customer service can be measured and give team members guidance on how particular elements of customer service are to be delivered day-to-day.

Examples might include:

- Telephones must be answered within two rings
- Emails must be answered the same working day
- Goods must be despatched within four hours
- Customers must not be left queuing for more than three minutes

What easily-measurable standards could you use in your business?

What standards do your direct competitors achieve, and what standards have customers come to expect from their dealings with other businesses?

USING INTERNAL INDICATORS

Not everything customers care about can be measured directly, but sometimes you can use information you have in your business to track progress.

What customer cares about	How you might measure it
Goods must be packaged well to avoid damage in transit	Broken returns
The business will get everything right first time	Complaints received
Effectiveness of the product or service you sell	Proportion of customers that buy again from you
Goods meet the customer's expectations	Number of returns under a no-quibbles money back guarantee
Your truck drivers are good road users and don't intimidate others	Number of complaints on your 'how's my driving?' toll-free phone line

STANDARDS AREN'T ENOUGH

Using standards and tracking company information can be helpful when you discover a particular problem in the company, perhaps because customers complain that you're always late or because the proportion of returns rockets.

But these standards are weak proxies for what you must really discover: **customer satisfaction**.

The risk is that by concentrating on a few easily measurable yardsticks, the business ignores other things that matter at least as much. The system fails, for example, if:

- A team member stops serving a customer in front of them because they must catch a phone before the second ring. The customer on the phone might be getting great service, but the one who's left waiting and is already mid-way through a transaction isn't

- A package is despatched within four hours to meet the deadline, but it's incomplete

Team members need to be empowered to respond to customers with common sense: to prioritise and take decisions about how to best satisfy customers.

CUSTOMER SATISFACTION

The best way to measure customer satisfaction is to ask customers how satisfied they are with your service, and ask them how it could be improved. You can do this by:

- Offering a freephone number they can call to recognise great service and complain about bad service
- Making customer service surveys easily available online
- Providing forms with a postage-paid envelope
- Following up on sales with a courtesy call to see how the customer is enjoying their purchase

Retail and restaurant chains often print the details of a phone or web survey on the back of the customer's receipt, and use a unique code so the feedback can be linked to the time of day, staff and product choice. Some shops provide simple yes/no buttons for customers to say whether the toilets were clean, or the service was prompt.

The easier you can make it, the more feedback you will get. Don't expect customers to invest a lot of time or money in helping you, and remember that the complaints might be more valuable than the praise because they help you to improve your service.

MEASURING SATISFACTION

The advantage of using satisfaction surveys is that they provide a way to measure how well you are meeting customer expectations, even though expectations vary from customer to customer. They also enable you to track changes in customer satisfaction over time.

You can ask customers to score how satisfied they are with your product quality out of 5, for example, and monitor the average score over time, and the number of people giving the top and bottom scores. You could break this data down by product, region or any other parameter.

The weakness is that the survey might not reflect everything customers care about. Provide space for customers to tell you anything and give you more detail on what went well, or not so well.

Surveys can overlook exceptional events too: remember that one terrible customer experience can have a huge impact online, even when most customers appear to be satisfied. Keep an eye on reviews and social media to see what customers are saying about you to others.

MYSTERY SHOPPER PROGRAMMES

Nearly every business can operate a mystery shopper programme, where researchers impersonate customers to gauge the level of service they receive. It can be run through any communication channel the company uses to deal with customers, such as by phone, in person or by email.

It's essential that team members don't know that the 'customer' is assessing them on behalf of the company. If you have a big organisation, the shoppers could be employees from other regions of the country, so they know the standards the company sets for customer satisfaction, and they can learn from the process too.

While the process will identify customer service shortfalls, it should also be used to reward those delivering exceptional service. Team members will feel uncomfortable with the process if it only seems to be there to spy on them.

MYSTERY SHOPPER PROGRAMMES

The advantage of running a mystery shopper programme is that it standardises the soft factors in customer service. A mystery shopper programme enables you to compare, for example, how friendly sales assistants are on a scale from one to five. Different team members, branches and departments can be measured against the same expectations.

The programme can also feed into company training initiatives. It will spot problems that customers might not tell you about.

Remember that all customers are different, and a successful mystery shopping trip doesn't guarantee that the next customer in the queue will leave satisfied. You still need to make it easy for customers to tell you how happy they are.

MYSTERY SHOPPER PROGRAMMES

REWARDING TEAM MEMBERS

Team members will be motivated by how you reward them. If they're paid a sales commission only, they are being encouraged to make as many sales of high-value items as possible. In some organisations this can lead to customers being dismissed quickly once the sale is in the bag or being mis-sold products.

It's inconsistent for companies to claim they put customer service first, but measure team performance by sales volume alone.

Make sure that your systems measure, recognise and reward great customer service. You could award a bonus based on customer satisfaction, for example.

REWARDING TEAM MEMBERS

You can reward good service given to you by colleagues by:

- Thanking them when they help you achieve your objectives. Everyone appreciates recognition for their work

- Giving them great service in return

MEASURING CUSTOMER SERVICE

CASE STUDY

At UK hi-fi retailer Richer Sounds, customers are given a customer service questionnaire with their receipt. The team member who makes the sale is rewarded with £5 if the customer ticks the box to say the service is excellent but is penalised £3 for service described as 'mediocre' and loses £5 if the service was 'poor'. Team members can earn £20 if customers write a letter of praise about their service, but lose £10 if someone writes to complain about them.

Staff aren't really fined if the balance is negative at the end of the month, although it would be a strong indicator that the team member is having problems and might benefit from extra training or more management support.

The store also runs a telephone survey (where friendliness counts for a quarter of the points) and a mystery shopper scheme.

For a scheme like this to work effectively, it's important that customers are not put under pressure to provide feedback or to give a positive rating.

PERSONAL
ACTION PLANNING

PERSONAL ACTION PLANNING

USING WHAT YOU HAVE LEARNED

Although it is sometimes interesting to learn new things just for their own sake, the pay-offs from a book like this one only come when you start to use your new knowledge and new skills in your day-to-day work. This is especially true of skills, which need to be practised regularly so that they become second nature, rather than something you have to think about doing deliberately.

So – are you now going out there to transform the way your organisation deals with customers? When you and the majority of your colleagues all start to make even small improvements in the quality of internal and external customer service, the cumulative impact soon becomes apparent.

Remember how you personally and the organisation as a whole benefit from great customer service.

PERSONAL ACTION PLANNING

REVIEW

This section is where you can look back over the main themes of this book to review what you have learned – and plan what you are going to do with it all.

Issues discussed in this book include:

- Why customer service matters
- How to delight customers
- How to communicate effectively with customers
- How to handle complaints from customers
- How to cooperate better with colleagues
- How to empower customer service in the organisation
- How to measure and reward great customer service

Skim through the book and make a list of anything you feel you could use in your job, either now or if other things changed to make it possible.

Be optimistic – go for it!

PERSONAL ACTION PLANNING

OVERCOMING OBSTACLES

If you've identified improvements you can make straight away, well done! You can start transforming your organisation now.

If you've identified improvements that will require change before you can make them, start thinking about how to effect the changes. Think about:

- What is getting in the way of making the improvements
- Whether these barriers are perceived or real
- Why these barriers exist
- Whether you can get around an obstacle
- Whether you can remove it
- Whether a colleague can help you tackle it, or is able to remove it entirely
- Whether somebody else is in a better position than you to make the improvement
- Who will benefit from the improvements, and how they can help them come about

You might find it helpful to discuss your ideas with colleagues. Winning their enthusiasm for the changes will make it easier to implement them and others will often have ideas that help you make things happen.

FURTHER INFORMATON

SUGGESTED READING

The Richer Way
by Julian Richer. Richer Publishing, 2009

Julian Richer reveals how putting people first has enabled him to build *Richer Sounds*, a business which entered the Guinness Book of Records for having the most profitable retail space.

Inside the Magic Kingdom: Seven Keys to Disney's Success
by Thomas K Connellan. Capstone, 1999

An entertaining story that reveals how attention to detail and customer service are part of everybody's job at Disney's theme parks.

Fish!
by Stephen C. Lundin, Harry Paul and John Christensen. Hodder paperbacks, 2002

Subtitled 'a remarkable way to boost morale and improve results' the book uses a story about a local fish market to show how poor internal relations in a large company can be transformed.

Wow! That's What I Call Service!
by Don Hales and Derek Williams. Ecademy Press, 2007

A collection of winning stories from the *WOW! Awards*, which were established to recognise exceptional customer service.

About the Authors

Sean McManus

Sean McManus writes inspiring books about business and technology. His books include Web Design in Easy Steps, iPad for the Older and Wiser, Microsoft Office for the Older and Wiser, and Raspberry Pi For Dummies. His magazine contributions have appeared in Marketing Week, Customer Loyalty Today and Business 2.0 among others. Visit his website at www.sean.co.uk for bonus content and free chapters from his books.

The late Tony Newby

Tony Newby, BA, MA, wrote the first edition of this popular guide to customer service in 1991, drawing on his extensive experience consulting and training in multinational and growing companies, as well as within local and central government. These assignments involved creating and delivering bespoke training courses, covering topics as diverse as culture change, assertiveness, creativity, effective listening, computer skills and customer service quality. His books on management training topics have been published in the UK and the USA.

Your details

Name _____

Position _____

Company _____

Address _____

_____

_____

Telephone _____

Fax _____

E-mail _____

VAT No. (EC companies) _____

Your Order Ref _____

Please send me:

			No. copies
The	Customer Service	Pocketbook	☐
The	_____	Pocketbook	☐
The	_____	Pocketbook	☐
The	_____	Pocketbook	☐

Order by Post
MANAGEMENT POCKETBOOKS LTD
LAUREL HOUSE, STATION APPROACH,
ALRESFORD, HAMPSHIRE SO24 9JH UK

Order by Phone, Fax or Internet
Telephone: +44 (0)1962 735573
Facsimile: +44 (0)1962 733637
Email: sales@pocketbook.co.uk
Web: www.pocketbook.co.uk

Customers in USA should contact:
Management Pocketbooks
2427 Bond Street, University Park, IL 60466
Telephone: 866 620 6944 Facsimile: 708 534 7803
Email: mp.orders@ware-pak.com
Web: www.managementpocketbooks.com

Pocketbooks – *available in both paperback and digital formats*

360 Degree Feedback*
Absence Management
Appraisals
Assertiveness
Balance Sheet
Body Language
Business Planning
Career Transition
Coaching
Cognitive Behavioural Coaching
Communicator's
Competencies
Creative Manager's
C.R.M.
Cross-cultural Business
Customer Service
Decision-making
Delegation
Developing People
Discipline & Grievance
Diversity*
Emotional Intelligence
Employment Law
Empowerment*
Energy and Well-being
Facilitator's
Feedback
Flexible Working*

Handling Complaints
Handling Resistance
Icebreakers
Impact & Presence
Improving Efficiency
Improving Profitability
Induction
Influencing
Interviewer's
I.T. Trainer's
Key Account Manager's
Leadership
Learner's
Management Models
Manager's
Managing Assessment Centres
Managing Budgets
Managing Cashflow
Managing Change
Managing Customer Service
Managing Difficult Participants
Managing Recruitment
Managing Upwards
Managing Your Appraisal
Marketing
Meetings
Memory
Mentoring

Motivation
Negotiator's
Networking
NLP
Nurturing Innovation
Openers & Closers
People Manager's
Performance Management
Personal Success
Positive Mental Attitude
Presentations
Problem Behaviour
Problem Solving
Project Management
Psychometric Testing
Resolving Conflict
Reward
Sales Excellence
Salesperson's
Self-managed Development
Starting In Management
Storytelling
Strategy
Stress
Succeeding at Interviews
Sustainability
Tackling Difficult Conversations
Talent Management

Teambuilding Activities
Teamworking
Telephone Skills
Telesales
Thinker's
Time Management
Trainer's
Training Evaluation
Training Needs Analysis
Transfer of Learning
Virtual Teams
Vocal Skills
Working Relationships
Workplace Politics
Writing Skills

* only available as an e-book

Pocketfiles

Trainer's Blue Pocketfile of
Ready-to-use Activities

Trainer's Green Pocketfile of
Ready-to-use Activities

Trainer's Red Pocketfile of
Ready-to-use Activities

To order please visit us at **www.pocketbook.co.uk**

09.08.1